FIRESIDE SERIES — Volume 2, No. 4

Ramtha

Everytime I have a thought that deals w/survival (jealousy, anger, hatred, depression, sadness, pain, insecurity, war, doubt, etc.) replace that thought w/ an image such as a lotus flower and build that image petal by petal until the flower is fully formed as an image in the brain. you will then unplug and replug your neuronets so that you don't think in terms of survival anymore you will think like a spiritual person instead of a human person and you will have greater mind. and be filled with abundance!

BUDDHA'S NEURONET FOR LEVITATION

OPENING THE LOTUS OF A THOUSAND PETALS

BUDDHA'S NEURONET FOR LEVITATION
OPENING THE LOTUS OF A THOUSAND PETALS
REVISED EDITION

Copyright © 2002, 2006 JZ Knight.

Cover design by Carmel Bartz

ISBN # 1-57873-066-X

JZK Publishing
Ramtha's School of Enlightenment
A Division of JZK, Inc.

P.O. Box 1210
Yelm, Washington 98597
360.458.5201
800.347.0439
www.ramtha.com
www.jzkpublishing.com

These series of teachings are designed for all the students of the Great Work who love the teachings of the Ram.

It is suggested that you create an ideal learning environment for study and contemplation.

Light your fireplace and get cozy. Prepare yourself. Open your mind to learn and be genius.

FOREWORD

The Fireside Series Collection Library is an ongoing library of the hottest topics of interest taught by Ramtha. These series of teachings are designed for all the students of the Great Work who love the teachings of the Ram. This library collection is also intended as a continuing learning tool for the students of Ramtha's School of Enlightenment and for everyone interested and familiar with Ramtha's teachings. In the last three decades Ramtha has continuously and methodically deepened and expanded his exposition of the nature of reality and its practical application through various disciplines. It is assumed by the publisher that the reader has attended a Beginning Retreat or workshop through Ramtha's School of Enlightenment or is at least familiar with Ramtha's instruction to his beginning class of students. This required information for beginning students is found in *Ramtha: A Beginner's Guide to Creating Reality*, Third Ed. (Yelm: JZK Publishing, a division of JZK, Inc., 2004).

We have included in the Fireside Series a glossary of some of the basic concepts used by Ramtha so the reader can become familiarized with these teachings. We have also included a brief introduction of Ramtha by JZ Knight that describes how all this began. Enjoy your learning and contemplation.

Contents

List of Figures

LOCALIZED STATES OF CONSCIOUSNESS IN THE BRAIN

Greetings, my beautiful masters. I salute you from the Lord God of my being to the Lord God of your being.

O my beloved Spirit,
Holy One,
your kingdom
and your power
omnipotent,
O my beloved Spirit,
I surrender unto you
my humble soul,
that you remake
and reconsider my destiny.
O my beloved Spirit,
that from creation
abide in my life
ever,
this I desire from you.
So be it.

Has it occurred to you that as we have discussed the brain in integral parts, each integral part accommodates a different state of consciousness? Wouldn't that make logic? Why have this huge, wonderful organism with all these different compartments in it if its only job is to run on premium gasoline? What if it can run on everything? What if each area of the brain is specifically tuned to specific areas of consciousness? For example, very gifted psychic people work from their midbrain. What is interesting here is that during their normal day's activities they are working from the yellow brain, the neocortex. It isn't until they start to do some sort of mundane work like cleaning up the dishes — such a mundane task that takes very little focus to do because it is a habit now — that while they are doing it they suddenly shift from yellow brain, which is now on automatic, into the midbrain. And while they are doing the most common of tasks, they suddenly get the most extraordinary information. You cannot be a psychic and be a focused intellectual. It doesn't work. They are not compatible with one another.

Psychics who are very gifted seem to be a little chaotic to the observer and almost a bit as if they were hypocrites because they go about using their yellow brain, they stumble around and they don't know the answers to certain things, and they go buy lotto cards and never win. A paradox, isn't it? They never win, but suddenly they can shift into a state of consciousness and know the most extraordinary things. Why aren't they consistent? Because they have never learned about the different areas of their brain, that is why. They don't know how states of consciousness are accelerated. No one does. So what happens is they walk around tending to their everyday life, just like you do, and when they try to use that ability, what part of the brain then are they trying to use the ability with? The yellow brain, the neocortex. Is the stream of consciousness that is accommodating the yellow brain going to be the same stream of consciousness that accommodates the midbrain? No.

That would mean then this ordinary person who has this extraordinary ability has never been taught to maintain that ability in a day-to-day situation because they literally cannot. How do you do the dishes in the future? In other words, if they walked around all day long in midbrain and took care of their tasks, then what they would be creating is the most boring and redundant future ever because they would be doing dishes, vacuuming, and cleaning the latrines in midbrain focus and high-band infrared, so that is what they are going to be doing in two weeks.

There is a lot to be said about the paradoxical behavior of gifted people. When they are put to the task of being tested, they nearly always fail the test. The skeptics rush in and say this person is a fraud, because when they are put to the test they are being put to the test in the applicable use of the yellow brain, and the yellow brain does not have the capacity that the midbrain does. If they had been disciplined and gained an enormous amount of knowledge and could learn to shift into different states of consciousness, they could actually shift into that midbrain upon command and in that state would never fail the tests. But fear, intimidation, being put on the spot — in other words, being spiritually weak because it has never been developed — they are always going to be made fun of and ridiculed. On the other hand, I expect one day for you to go through the most rigorous testing that MIT[1] has. You are going to learn the difference between states of consciousness so when you do move into them, the flow is with you, and the moment you move out of it you will feel when you have moved out of it.

Doing Fieldwork[SM] and focusing on the Void[2] has much greater application than simply learning to get your card off the fence. The greater applications are learning to define altered states of consciousness and to be able to access them.

In brain science, different parts of the brain register different frequencies. The states that the brain moves into in frequency are alpha, beta, theta, and delta. That is a little contraire to science, but if you apply what you have learned to the different sections of the brain and map it, you will be able to understand why I put it in the order that I did.

---

1 Massachusetts Institute of Technology in Cambridge, Massachusetts was founded in 1865. This world-renowned university is famous for its leading scientific research. It was one of the first schools to introduce the laboratory as a teaching method.
2 Any of the disciplines of the Great Work designed and taught by Ramtha.

If science in its Stone Age technology can measure brain-wave activity through this primitive source, that should also tell you that the brain then is operating off of some sort of gear system. When you shift the gears, the reason the frequency changes is because it is accommodating a stream of consciousness. This is not conventional science. Conventional science wants to contain the brain as being the creator of consciousness. They get confused as to what consciousness is, what the mind is, and what the brain is, but somehow the brain is responsible for springing all of this phenomenon to force. The idea in modern-day science that there are levels of consciousness streaming into the brain and that it is essentially a receiver/transmitter then begins to make a lot of sense as to why the brain behaves in the modulated forms of frequency that it does. When they get brave enough to actually admit that, even though they have no proof, it will help to explain a plethora of human misery.

BUILDING SUPPLIES FOR THE MONUMENTAL PALACE CALLED YOUR LIFE

The yellow brain is a gift and damnation. It is a gift because it is a huge amount of territory that still lies dormant in you. You use less than a tenth of your brain, so what is going on in the rest of it? Is anyone home? Evolution has this sort of attitude that if you don't use it you are going to lose it, such as what happened to your little toe and the other one that used to be there and why you don't have a lot more body hair than you used to. Evolution says that the environment and your attitude towards it dictate biological change in the organism, so why haven't you lost your big brain? If you use less than a tenth of it, then why do you still have it? It is certainly burdensome unless, of course, it is there strictly to hang your face on and to grow hair. The yellow brain, when properly used, will produce an utter God because the yellow brain, besides taking over the burden of the functioning of the body in different elements, has also got vast office space for rent and for lease. This is because the yellow brain is supposed to be the organ inside of you that collects data, in other words, knowledge.

The yellow brain is there as a vast computer ready for input so that it can store that input. The yellow brain already is sitting on the greatest treasure, the midbrain. It can never be improved upon, except developed. It is already the best it will ever be. This yellow throne is sitting on the most fabulous resource that will ever be created. It is sitting up there to house more memory. The reason it needs to do that is because the more knowledge that you have about everything, the greater neural links you have to build from that knowledge new paradigms or new models of thoughts. Those new models of thought are what are going to create the future timeline.

If you don't gather knowledge, you are walking around impoverished. Think of knowledge in terms of tools and building supplies for the great architect, which are the midbrain and the lower cerebellum. The great architect wants to build a palatial cathedral for your life, using that as the analogy for an outrageously divine, historical monument — your life. Then it goes upstairs to the storage room, which has got a lot of rats running around and cobwebs hanging around, and now that it has the design, it is endeavoring to see what kind of building materials it has. So what does it find?

How much do you know about anything? In other words, what sort of knowledge do you have sitting up here that a God could pull from, like a giant puzzle — take a little from this section and a little from this section and a little from that section — and then putting it together starts to lay the foundation of the great cathedral, that everything that you need is there, and this God then starts to lay the foundation and build. What kind of building materials would it need? It would obviously have to be a rich quarry of stone, marble, and alabaster, a rich quarry, and that the God could mine out of that quarry everything that it needs to build this beautiful place.

Let's say then instead of limestone, alabaster, and marble, let's substitute those for variant knowledge. How much knowledge do you have about quantum mechanics, how much knowledge do you have about subatomic fields, or do you even care? Subatomic fields are the invisible foundations to all life. Subatomic fields are not only particles but energy and they explain how matter comes together through the Observer. How much of that do you know? If you don't know a lot, then what is going to happen is the ability to instigate an immediate access to probable tools has just been eliminated because the source for all the building tools is going to be the subatomic realm. If you don't know anything about that, then that is one place you are going to be weak and that you can't mine. And what is going to happen? You are going to say, "Well, I don't have any."

Your God is going to say to you, "Then how do you expect us to give you a future that is a renaissance of your own genius lying latent? How are we going to give you a fabulous life if you don't even have within your brain the acceptability and the building materials to make it?"

You can say, "Well, I don't have that but I have a lot of relationship studies over here. I know how to build men and women statues for the outside of the doors."

"That is it?"

"Well, that is it."

How much do you know about physics? Even though it is boring to you, don't you think that if it is the integral building stones to whatever desire you want that it is time you learned about them? You do not have to be a mathematician because all math is, is the language to describe what it is.

Then the next time I say to you we are going to dissolve your past, you would look at me and know exactly what I am talking about. The past to you are neuronet models that sit up here in your brain that keep holding together your present and current life. Guilt, shame, inadequacy, all the things that you have difficulties with, keep your life together right now, even right down to the people in your life. So when I say to you we are going to change your past and we are going to dissolve it, you would know I am saying that we are going to unplug the neuronet of the past and reserve all of its resources of wisdom. We are going to unplug it and let it dissolve.

What you would see immediately and with total acceptance is that the energy patterns that hold together all these people in your life, all these problems in your life, and all these inadequacies in your life, you would know that the moment the Observer erases the program of the neuronet then the whole world around you crumbles apart and dissolves. You would know that because you would understand how the quantum field of particle science works. Then you would look at me and say, "I am ready. So be it." What you would say if you didn't know that would be, "Well, I trusted you." Trust me? Why would you want to do that? Why wouldn't you want to trust yourself? I am your teacher. Why should I carry your burden of trust? Don't you think you should carry it? Now that is being a God.

If I said to you I am going to dissolve your past and you don't know anything about how this field operates, you know what is going to happen to you? There is going to be a fear arise in your neuronet, a fear of losing something. That causes confusion and causes you to grip even tighter to your attitudes in your subconscious. And what happens when they are focused upon? They become the dominant theme in your brain for days and you can't stop thinking about it. You start crying, you are worried, you are gnashing your teeth, biting your fingernails off to where you have none, and you are eating the town that you live in. I see it all the time.

Is not fear the root of survival? Even the most miserable people, I swear to you, they walk around miserable, but the day you said, "I will dissolve your past and abolish it," they would kill you.

They say, "I have an eating disorder."

"You do? Well, why don't you let me send you a runner and we will get it unplugged." They hate you. They don't want to unplug it. They just want to brag about it.

So miserable people, even though we have the solution to the problem in their life and we have the extraordinary wisdom on how to correct it, would rather have misery than the unknown. They prefer sadness over relief, and they will work really hard to change everything in their life, no matter if it is stuck in a certain position because it is the only way it could stay. They will learn to switch them around by moving them around on the pallet of their table, and they just take this attitude and move it over here and say, "There, I feel so much better." The attitude is still there. They move it around but never abolish it.

If you are going to really be the masters of superconsciousness, you must be the masters of time. That includes the burden of one's past, because the past is like wearing old clothes that you never change and yet you wonder why you smell bad all the time. Your past ekes the same smell, and you wear it thickly.

If your yellow brain needs to create a new future for yourself, it needs resources in which to do that. The yellow brain is a gigantic empty office space waiting to be filled up with libraries of knowledge. You should study quantum mechanics, absolutely. Do it. You should study a foreign language. You should learn to play instruments because it helps to develop the right and the left simultaneously in the brain. You should learn as much as you can about the brain, about the cells, about hormones. What you don't know, you go read and find out and you make notes and study them, and you do it just the way that I teach you here. You draw at the end of your study a cartoon to describe what you just learned. If you do that, now your brain is getting rich.

The yellow brain so far has an impoverished amount of knowledge. It is only possessed by your habits. You use it to conform to daily ritual. That is all you use it for. You use it for your sexuality, you use it for your appearance, you use it for your image, but you don't use it for knowledge and you don't use it to change your life. If the only tools that you have are how to look good, smell good, and eat good, if that is all you have got up here in your brain, what sort of palace are we going to be able to build for you? That is the great architect's dilemma.

Keep in mind that the more you know, the more ignorance you abolish, and the more ignorance that you abolish, the greater your level of acceptance and belief in what you are doing. What that means is that according to the yellow brain, your ability to accept a destiny is only equal to how much you believe in it, and how much you believe in it is only equal to how much you know about it.

People do not have a great tendency to accept that which is unknown to them. Most people don't like to admit that they have a very narrow band of acceptance, but most everyone does. We can readily manifest within the realm of what you accept. Easy, no problem. If we go outside of that, we have difficulty. You now understand then the necessity for gaining knowledge in substantial amounts. When I talk to you about abolishing your past, you understand it from a structural point of view and a neural point of view, so the understanding is not accompanied by a fear of loss. When we do, we can remold it into something much greater than what you have been used to.

Neurobiology of a Thought

If the yellow brain is the predominant area for language, deciphering the senses and putting that into language description, it is also the seat of attitude, so we are going to understand what attitudes are.

Let's go to this drawing here. Nerve cells sort of look like a squid, lots of little squids in the brain.

FIG. 1: NERVE CELL CONNECTIONS

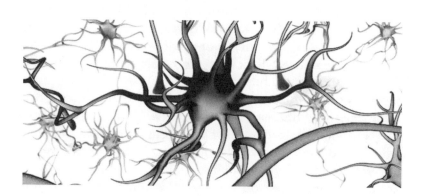

Dendrites are docking stations for other neurons and other nerve cells. Here we have drawn three nerve cells that are interconnected, and we are going to use this as a study model of neurosynaptic patterning in the brain.

FIG. 2: NEURONS FIRING AND THE SYNAPTIC CLEFT

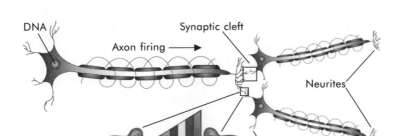

Firing at different
levels of quantum potential

If all the nerve cells are firing at the neurosynaptic cleft, what is the point of having all of them connected to one another if all they are doing is firing? Would it just be a lightning storm in the brain? What is it about this characterization of neurons and their populace that brings about the hologram in the brain? Do you assume that because this nerve cell creates a magnetic flux on the outside and the inside of the axon — it is actually sending a spark down its axon — that when the spark goes out each one of these tendrils of these neurons that it will be the same spark going out of all of them? In other words, are they all accommodating the same spark, as spark plugs do?

The axon of a nerve cell has little tiny gates on it that open and close. The resting charge inside of a nerve cell is positive because it has more positive molecules in it than it does on the outside. On the outside it has more negative. The arm of the nerve cell, the axon, is so long because it is actually a chemical factory and it has all of these negative and positive particle charges inside of it. In its resting state, when it is not firing with its neurons, it has a net positive charge. It is an electrical entity.

What creates the momentum of the charge down the arm of the axon is that around it flowing in liquid, the fluid in the brain, there are also charged particles but their net resting state is negative. So we have resting positive, resting negative. Along the arm there are these little tiny cattle gates and for every gate that opens up, there is a gate that lets out. There is a gate for these particles on the outside to flow into the arm and there are gates for the particles inside of the arm to flow out.

When the soma and the nuclei convulse an electrical charge in its nucleus — it is like lightning over its membrane — the spark lights up down the arm. The only way that spark can travel is if the net electrical charges are countered on either side, which means as soon as the charge starts, the gates open and allow the negative particles to flow in and, simultaneously, another gate is opening to let the positive flow out. Now we are getting electricity. We are getting an electrical current moving and oscillating around this arm. As these little minute gates are opening, according to metabolism, letting positive flow out and negative flow in, the spark then, like rotating electricity, is moving down the arm and then it travels out the neuron.[3] As this charged spark travels out of the neuron, it fires and releases serotonin enzymes. While it fires, a dendrite picks up the neurotransmitter from an accommodating nerve cell. There is an exchange going on. As this electrical charge moves down the arm, the gates start to close back up behind it. The arm is returning

3 The spark is moving down the axon of the neuron toward the dendrite connections of another nerve cell at the synaptic cleft. See fig. 2.

then to what is called a net positive resting state and a net negative state flowing around it as the charge moves down the arm.

We are endeavoring to explain a science here that even the greatest neuroscientists have a great amount of difficulty explaining, because they really don't know how the neurons in their subsequent firing activity can produce a holographic picture. They don't understand how that could work. Demonstrating this to you now on such a simple level allows you to gain enough knowledge to begin to connect the idea of how it is possible.

LEVITATION — A CHANGE IN THE RESONANT FIELD

Taking the next step after we understand how the neuron emits a charge, we are going to take a look at the charge itself.

Master of Music, you answer this question. This is what B-flat looks like as a sound wave.[4] What happens if we take the sound wave and it goes from looking like that on the right to this on the left? What has caused it to do that?

Music: It would be a change in frequency.

Ramtha: To what?

Music: To a lower frequency.

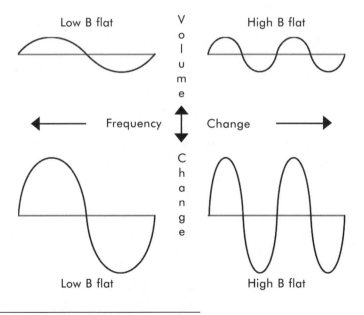

FIG. 3: FREQUENCY CHANGE CHART

---

4 See fig. 3.

Ramtha: Is it still B-flat?

Music: I don't think so.

Ramtha: What would it be?

Music: Another harmonic.

Ramtha: But is it the same B-flat?

Music: Well, this is an octave higher, but it would be a B-flat.

Ramtha: So this is really B-flat? Is that what you are telling me, Master of Music?

Music: I guess.

Ramtha: You guess? We have taken a sound, a tone, and we have exaggerated it. Does this mean that it is louder or does it mean it is a different frequency? It is not the same frequency. If you think that it is, then would you explain the paradox to me. It is B-flat and it is louder, but is it the same frequency? Because it becomes louder means that its frequency beat has changed.

Here is the reason why this is important, and it has a complication about it, a paradox. When we discuss in this outrageous school the possibility of you levitating, levitation no longer is a myth but becomes an integral part of our philosophy. If we talk about it in terms of philosophy, you can be certain that anytime I start to discuss it that there is going to be a way to accomplish it. Theoretically when an entity levitates, it is because they have changed the resonant field of their bands. They are actually encased in a bubble of frequency that is greater than the time/space dimension that they are presently existing in. To make that a little simpler, that would mean that everyone sitting next to you is vibrating at the same rate that you are. They are all B-flat. No matter how enlightened you think you are, if you can see and touch and smell that person, they are B-flat. Now that means that they are resonating the same as the field of matter in this time resonates.

If we are to accept a philosophy as outrageous as levitation, we have to change some conventional views. We have to change them because if we don't, we will never get to levitate. This is true genius. I will teach you how to levitate once we have worked on your focus. What you would start to do is you would alter the resonant field that you are currently in.

Let's interject something here before it slips from me. Remember this in any literature that you read about field phenomenon. Field phenomenon is sort of like radiation, microwave fields, electromagnetic fields. Listen to me very carefully. All fields are a product of a stream of consciousness. They are the phenomenon of consciousness. Now with that in mind, then all fields known and unknown are subject to streams of consciousness. And what is the greatest accelerator that you now possess that can tune into different streams of consciousness? The brain. Keep that in mind.

To learn to levitate is to change the resonant frequency field that you currently inhabit. That would mean if you are B-flat here on the top of the chart and we started having you resonate like the bottom of the chart, you would still be B-flat but your frequency would change. Your frequency is getting louder. In other words, we are changing your resonant frequency. You are still B-flat because we can still touch you and see you, but we are going to accelerate that field. We are going to make the field loud, not that you can hear but that you can see, and so the frequency is going to be different but you are still B-flat. It is a paradox. But if you don't accept this paradox, even though it is contraire to physical science, then you will never experience what they don't know.

We are not going to work within the frames of accepted thought here because you wouldn't want me to do that to you. We are going beyond what science doesn't even know yet. But given that then, you would learn to accelerate your resonant field. What that does to the bands is it puts them in a magnetic flux. When they do that, they are actually gravity-eaters. The field is antigravity because it is not resonating at B-flat any longer. It is resonating at a higher, louder harmonic, thereby consuming gravity and allowing the entity to lift off and sit there. It is actually eating the B-flat fields around you and taking them into a vortex of energy, which allows antigravity to exist and brings upon the state of levitation.

Now here is another paradox. Why did I say that the resonant field created by altering the resonant field eats gravity? Why would I say that? Why would I say that the new field created from B-flat — although it is changed it is still B-flat — why did I make that outlandish comment? Why does it eat gravity? Here is a clue. Yeshua ben Joseph, when he appeared on the mount before his crucifixion, appeared with some very famous fellows from antiquity. He was recorded being seen with them.[5] Do you remember who they were? Well, it is a long time ago. You cannot even remember what happened thirty-two days ago at 10:00 A.M. in the morning. I do believe the name of the chap was Elijah, and Moses, and Jacob. So he made an interesting comment to his poor ignorant disciples. He said, "Now don't touch me."

And they said, "Well, why not? You are glowing."

He said, "I am presently of this world but I am not in this world."

"You are of this world but you are not in this world?"

That should keep us busy for two thousand years. What he was saying was that he had created an alternate field, and because he did he zipped on into another dimension in which he could talk to fellows that he was in agreement with and in which there was not anything like time here. That is the reason why he could talk to these supposedly dead and resurrected entities, because even though you could see him he wasn't in this world. The reason that he said, "Don't touch me" is "because I will eat your energy if you do because I am vibrating so fast that I am eating time

5 Jesus' transfiguration story: see Gospel according to Mark 9, 2-8, Matthew 17, 1-8, Luke 9, 28-36; and Jesus' appearance to Mary Magdalene after his resurrection, John 20, 11-18.

and space by virtue of occupying the space that I am presently in."

B-flat is able to be B-flat because it has a certain field. It is paying rent to live there. It is leasing that time and space in order to be B-flat. The moment that it changes and becomes a rotating field — completely bizarre, even though it is still itself — it eats everything around it because everything around it is getting to occupy that space it is in by paying duty to gravity. When it changes, it eats all of the gravity around it because its space is vibrating higher than the lower space in which it previously occupied. In order for it to blow up and exist in this same time, though not be of this time, it is eating the time it is presently in.

So what happens if suddenly you are no longer sitting in a gravitational field? What if suddenly the Earth's pull on you was released, what would happen to you? Is that theoretically possible? It happens every day. When you change your resonant frequency, you alter the field in which you are in and the field becomes pliable according to focused consciousness. That field, overlapped in this field, will be an antigravity field because it will eat gravity to sustain its higher resonance.

Hidden Symbolism of the Levitating Buddha and the Lotus Flower

When I tell you that the brain is interdimensional, the brain has this fabulous characteristic of being able to exist in many worlds simultaneously because it is a conductor of that which is termed resonant field energy. When I say to you if your yellow brain could fire pictures in the frequency of infrared, we could see how thoughts are actually levitations of the future because they are existing as a real time here and now but have their frequency in another world, whose other world becomes the progenitor of the future.

We have just discussed the viable science of levitation that allows you, as a heavy three-dimensional object vibrating according to the hertz of the planet, to have the same stability as mass itself. If suddenly you were to change your field, then the mass that you are made up of would change as well. You would still be you but you would be vibrating at another frequency. By doing that then you would still be in the world but not of the world. In other words, we can see you and you are still John Doe, but you are not in the world because you are no longer obeying the laws of gravity and physics here. So you are actually levitating fifteen feet above the floor. We can see you but you are eating the surrounding time in this time. And while you are sitting there, you are actually in the future. You are in another dimension of time that will one day be your linear future.

If that is then plausible and theoretically possible, then we are discussing a whole new model here, that the sign of the floating Buddha above the lotus flower is not just some beautiful mantra or mandala to be able to study. It is actually an encoded symbolism that is showing you that with that state of intense focus, you can levitate. But what does the symbol of the Buddha floating above the lotus flower represent? That the Buddha is living now an immortal timeline. What he is doing is floating there but he is actually living thousands of years into the future, because although he is seen five thousand years ago he still has two more thousand years to go in his timeline.

It also represents the thought of the Buddha, whose symbolism was that he was sitting there in absolute peace defying the laws of gravity. He also represented a thought, a constructed thought, and that the highest form of thought sits in the brain in absolute peace. It is called the third eye, and the Buddha represented the third eye. What he was actually saying to us in mute symbolism was that everything you think is equal to the levitating Buddha. If I have a person in this school who can levitate fifteen feet off the floor, then everyone else meditating around that person is the same with that entity, because to construct a thought that is also antigravity working in high-band infrared is equal to the Buddha or equal to you floating in a nongravity field, because thought is the same thing as the Buddha.

The Buddha represented that thoughts created architecturally live in a timeline far into the distant future, and though the thoughts cannot be seen in your head from the outside it is because they are living in a future dimensional time in an antigravity field. Given that then, we would understand why that thought fired appropriately and consistently is actually a Buddha or an archetype that starts to levitate. When it does, it is levitating in high-band infrared, which is way out there in the future casting its shadow down this way. That thought then, as it falls, starts to manipulate energy and collapse it into particles to create the form here. So levitation is equal to what the yellow brain can do best with the support of the midbrain.

Then you say, "Wait a minute. You are saying that my thoughts are levitating?" Exactly. But you know why you haven't levitated? Because you didn't know your thoughts were levitating. Now that you know that they do, it changes the whole idea of your flexibility in time because the brain projects a thought in infrared frequency — it is creating B-flat to resonate at a loud sound wave — and the thought's model sits up here above the head. The head is actually projecting it. It is levitating above your head. Nobody can see it. But if you were in the infrared band you could see it, and it is levitating. And what it is doing if held there for a period of time is that it starts to eat the gravitational field around it. What does that mean to you? That means that an idea can eat up your past.

Think of it this way, because we are going to get into the science of the neurons and how they accomplish this magnanimous feat. If the brain is firing through millions of neurons a spark, each spark is like a chord on the harp when strummed. It resonates, and the sum total produces a picture that is holographic, that can be analyzed in three-dimensional terms. The brain has the capacity to do that. Where is the hologram taking place? Where is the projected hologram's destiny? You think it is in the head but it is actually above the head.

So as you are walking across the field focusing on your card,[6] if you are doing it correctly you are creating a hologram that is occupying the same resonant field as a levitating master occupies when he is levitating. The only difference between the thought-form as a hologram and the levitating master is that with the levitating master, you touch them beside you, you feel them, but they start to change their resonant frequency. They are eating gravity. You can still see them. You can't see a thought but it is there and so it occupies the same gravitational field that a levitating master does, and they are sitting side by side. The idea of the Buddha levitating above the lotus was to show you that the thought of the Buddha is in levitation as well.

You can still see the master but he glows. He can seem of this world because he still looks like the person you

---

6 Practicing the discipline of Fieldwork[SM].

know, but he is not in this world because he is now living in high-band infrared. His image remains but it only remains as it feeds upon the time-flow it just left.

The reason why a single thought can change your life if concentrated on long enough is that if you levitate a thought up here, as we studied, the way that the brain works is it works in the future-Now. So we construct a hologram and we put it right up there and it is levitating. What it does to you, held for a long period of time, is it also feeds off of the time-frame dimension. So what would the thought's field start feeding on? It would start feeding on the gravity around it. And what is the gravity around it? Your past.

Now we are about to describe in physical terms how this outrageous concept is accomplished, and it is going to solve many problems that arise when you start reading books on the brain, which I want you to do. When you start to come to this area, remember our discussion. Remember how we discussed the neurons firing, the collective neuronet, the holographic images, and that they are not inside of the brain but are actually projected above the head itself. Understand that they are in high-band infrared. Understand all of it because you are not going to read this anywhere else, but what you read you will be able to fill in with what you have learned here. You will be exceedingly happy that you learned this as well as what your future is going to look like in this school, fifteen feet off of the ground.

The reason that the ancient Buddhists used the lotus flower of many petals as their focused meditation was that they would start with the bud and then they would slowly start to unfold each one of its many petals. The focused meditation upon the thousand-petal lotus flower, focused upon intently and repetitively day after day, brought about enlightenment. Interesting that a flower should bring about enlightenment, but what is it that they are trying to tell us over the ages through symbolism? Simply this, that if a student of the mind works every day in the mind unfolding the petals of a lotus and then the lotus gets greater and greater and greater, there is a promise that in the center of the lotus will be found the jewel of the lotus. What they were trying to get everyone to do — which is the truth — is that every day when they did this, they started out with a little neuronet, a little idea occupying a little space above their head. The next day they did it they went a little further. They counted more petals and held the vision above their head. The next day they did it they went further and counted more petals. It took them about two years to be able to count a thousand petals in visual meditation.

FIG. 4: MANTRA OF AVALOKITESHVARA:
OM MANI PADME HUM — BEHOLD, THE JEWEL IN THE LOTUS

So above the head starts the bud. Every day the student was to open the lotus, and when they could fully open a thousand petals there would appear a jewel. In order to accomplish that task, you call upon the extraordinary brain to be able to do that. In order for the brain to project the image of a hundred petals is going to require a hundred thousand neurons firing to accomplish that. If we get a thousand petals counted, how many more neurons are we going to need? You know how to multiply or to square it? An enormous amount. So why are we going to find a jewel at the end of a thousand petals? Because creating the hologram of a thousand-petal lotus will take a trillion neurons to accomplish.

Isn't that eating the past away, because where are you going to get the rest of those neurons to accomplish a thousand-petal task? Aren't you going to have to run over here to your right brain and start borrowing out of insecurity?

Can you imagine running over here and flinging open the trunk and pulling these things out?

"Insecurity: Here, you can have this. Envy, jealousy: Oh, here, you can have it. War, doubt. Here is war, but I really like doubt. Success, right over here. Failure, there is another suitcase over here. Ah, let's see, what have I got left? Lack, a little prejudice. Lots of lack."

"We need a little more."

"Here, here, let's see. Ah, that is it, pain. Here, you can have this. I have nothing else left. Go in there and take anything you want. I don't care. It is yours."

"Just what I wanted to hear."

Do we understand the mystery of meditating on the thousand-petal lotus? The jewel that opens up has completely eaten your past as its field grows by unplugging your neuropathways to your personality and your past. The jewel is God, totally open. Imagine this thousand-petal lotus levitating up here has eaten all of your past, has taken every part of your personality to develop the neuropathway to create an outstanding neuronet vision in high-band infrared, and it is now casting the shadow to the future. What would the future be but God? Isn't that what the Buddha is?

Each nerve cell with its subsequent neurons coming off the axon is a specialist in degrees of delivering the frequency of the spark that it has. Each nerve cell in the brain is a little different. Its atomic biology is slightly changed from its neighbor. That means that each minute neuron has the capacity to deliver a different phase of the same spark. Think of phases of a spark. If we think of the spark as a wall, we would think of phases then as the different cut stones that build that wall. Then each neuron is a specialist in phases. When the color yellow is needed, the phase of yellow harmonic is a specialized group of neurons that knows how to fire that phase in order to give that color. We begin to see how all the soldiers of the brain are actually specialists in their ability to deliver that fire. When they deliver the fire, they are representing a photon fraction of an entire picture. They are projecting from their particular specialty a phase of frequency that when all are put together create an image.

It is as simple as this. If all the neurons in the brain phased at the same time or gave the same frequency spark, then you would just have a plain whiteout. There would be no definition, hue, color, or depth. It takes each one of these neurons to deliver their specialty at phase/frequency firing in order to give the picture three-dimensional life and integrity.

Then we see the brain is even more marvelous and that in the yellow brain, containing all of these nerve cells, each one of these neurons is going to phase differently according to the charge that comes through the axon. These phases could be higher, lower, in-between, slower, and louder. If you see how we have these nerve cells hooked up, we have each of these hooked up to different parts of each other and we see that each neuron is actually helping its neighbor in phasing.

WHEN SURVIVAL IS OUR MOTIVATION RATHER THAN EVOLUTION

Now in all of the universe you have to be regarded as the specialists in emotional neuropathways. Emotional neuropathways are what we originally talked about when we started this discussion on the brain, that the brain's main job is the survival of the total organism. Under survival there is a main switching bank in the brain, like a plug-in. All of these emotions — pain, insecurity, fear, war, doubt, success, failure, lack, prejudice — you accumulated from the time that you were born. These fundamentally represent what started the foundation of your personality, and all of it starts out under the code of survival, all of it does.

If we then take these three neurons as a microcosm,[7] then we can see that all of these particular attitudes were created because they represent neuropathways that fundamentally were created to allow survival to continue. If you use survival as the explanation point, go through these attitudes in your mind, hook them up to survival,[8] and say, "Insecurity, why would I be insecure? Because I don't like to take risks. Why don't I want to take risks? Because I am afraid for my survival." If you can accept that, then you will begin to see how the fundamental aspects of the weakness of your personality have been developed.

Don't you find that a little enlightening about yourself? Furthermore, if what you are afraid of is that you are not going to survive, these wicked emotions always kick in and always become very foreboding for the entity to have to live through. Yet it is also part and parcel the responsibility

---

7 See fig. 2.
8 The list of attitudes written on the board: "Pain, insecurity, fear, war, doubt, success, failure, lack, prejudice."

of the brain to do this to protect the organism. It is sort of, as nature would say, the survival of the fittest. So if we use that term then and go down these attitudes, we can see how all of them become viable.

Every one of these attitudes takes up an enormous amount of neuronet. Whether you realize it or not, everything you do is connected into their ground level — everything. So if we were to trace back every choice you have made, every statement you have made, and everything you have done, we could take every one of those back to these fundamental neuronet bases. Don't you find that a little disturbing that instead of being motivated by love, you are motivated by survival? When it comes to survival, your skin will always be the most important skin around and you will sell out any moral judgment for the sake of being in a survival mode. I tell you it is one of humanity's greatest downfalls and why in the slow wheels of reincarnation it takes so long to become an enlightened master, because everyone is willing to sell out for the sake of their daily bread. I find it appalling.

The true martyrs of antiquity were those who didn't sell out, those who didn't turn gray and were diplomats. They were indeed, even though they were outrageous, refreshing winds upon a stagnated civilized culture that brought about true controversy and stirred the pot and broke up that smooth veneer that hides all these wicked attitudes.

I like very much the saying, "What gain a man if he gain the entire world and lose his soul?" What has he gained, and is it possible to lose your soul? Well, it sort of is, because if you do not arise to the soul agenda that is provided to you through reincarnation and sell it out for the simple conviction of surviving, you do lose in a lifetime. When you really know and the number is up and you have to come back and look at all of this, you know then that what you did was live through the covenant of the flesh instead of the covenant of the Spirit.

The Spirit is none of these attitudes and we can

understand how it couldn't be, because if the Spirit is here to make known the unknown, what is unknown about these? How could a Spirit that is omnipotent be jealous of itself? How could a Spirit that is all-powerful be possibly in lack? How could a Spirit hate? What is there to hate? It doesn't need to survive. It is that which survival comes from.

Your Spirit is the ultimate moralist. Moreover, your Spirit is the unlimited, outrageous aspect of yourself that has nothing to do with survival but has everything to do with the engines that fire evolution, because the engines that fire evolution are indeed the ability to make known the unknown. That is its agenda, but humans are squabbling for their daily bread and using all of these scurrilous techniques in order to scoot on by. It is in all of you.

What becomes problematic in regard to this and the teachings is that this occupies an enormous part of your life. Remember I talked about the hunger of the Spirit and how you never miss a meal but you starve to death your Spirit? Well, that is sort of the problem here. You are so involved with your humanity and the neuronet of your humanity that you are starving your Spirit. We have to go to such extremes as to teach you to sit still and focus on a blooming lotus until you have manufactured a thousand petals out of it visually. Only until we can do that does the Spirit dominate the brain and abolish the humanity. Why do we want to do that? Because if your goal is to be an unlimited, outrageous, miraculous, immortal being, then you have to get rid of this because it will undermine everything you do. Moreover, you will start focusing for the sake of survival instead of the sake of evolution. Did you know that when you focus for the sake of survival you are coming from an energy of lack instead of abundance?

Now listen to this terrifying message. If you are focusing for the need of survival, what is going to come up immediately in your life? Let's go down the list: pain, insecurity, fear, war, doubt, success, failure, lack, prejudice. Does this sound familiar? The moment you started focusing on something that you really needed, all of a sudden out of nowhere comes the emotional body, like a marching army, beheading and slicing everything in its path. You woke up ugly and mad and you didn't even know why. You kicked the cat, you fired the cook, you had a flat tire. Where did this stuff come from? You, because this is fundamentally tied into survival. So when you start focusing on need, it means you are in lack. It is tied in with all these other things over here in survival. Your neuronet, in order to survive, started firing up that which it is tied into, so your anger is explained. Instead of being happy for your friend's prosperity, you give them lip service. You say, "I am really happy and proud of you," and underneath you hate their guts. They don't deserve this. What did they do to deserve that? You are jealous of them, you secretly hate them, and where did all of this come from? This came from survival. So anytime you start focusing on manifesting something that you need, you are going to bring this picture up, and this explains why.

We don't have enough years to go into the scope and the magnitude of this harassment, but it is man- and woman-made, and it is because of survival, and it is because you sell out for what you need instead of what you know.

Unplugging Undesired Emotional Neuropathways

That is why Yeshua ben Joseph said, "Listen, if your eye continues to see evil, pluck it out. If your arm continues to do vile things, cut it off. If your legs keep running to the bars, cut them off." Unfortunately, a lot of monks after that took him real seriously, and so castration became the order of the day because their penises violated them and they just cut them off. That took care of that problem.

What is meant here is that you unplug these neuronets. And so efficient is your brain that when you start to focus on something, it shifts into gear and that neuronet starts to play. What does that look like? It is sitting right up there in three dimensions in infrared. Isn't that wonderful? It is firing all of those things. They are sitting up here and casting a shadow on your future, and instead of getting what you need, you get a lot of guff.

We want to unplug them. We want to cut them off. We want to deal with them, but how do you deal with that? The Buddhists had a wonderful solution: Sit and focus on blooming a thousand-petal lotus blossom. A crazy Westerner would scratch his head and say, "What in the world does that have to do with insecurity?" and the Buddhist says, "Everything."

Why do we have him do that? Because sooner or later if he was really sincere in changing, he would create a thought hologram that would consume the field around it and consume the neuronet in order to finish the vision. What does that look like? It just starts to unplug. Slowly and surely it starts to get unplugged.

Now science has proven through time-lapse photography that when a new thought is overlaid consistently, these little neurons at the synaptic cleft of the dendrite start to shrivel away and hook up somewhere else until they are finally plugged in. What happens is that we have to unplug this neuronet. No master can tolerate these attitudes sitting in their brain. They do that by creating focused thought that they have carefully thought out, that the moment a familiar thought comes in they replace it with one of the following visions. The moment they start thinking frantic or in lack, they know it.

As lack begins to appear as an emotion, they replace it with a new thought and they keep focusing on it until this gets unplugged. Then slowly the emotional body starts to subside. Then the next time they start to feel jealous or envious, they have already got a lotus flower vision prepared. The next time they start to feel that, as they start to get emotionally enraged, they start focusing on this card or on this thought-form. They are forcing their brain to unplug and move into building this cathedral, and as they build, the emotional body starts to subside. They may have to do that for thirty days, but at the end of thirty days they will have finally resolved the neuronet conflict into wisdom. It will be permanently unplugged in the brain and will be kept only as wisdom, because the wisdom is contained in the hippocampus as long-term memory. There is no longer a fundamental daily working part of the mental apparatus of the human being here. Slowly we start to unplug all of these attitudes, and as we unplug all of them we replace them with new models and we force the neuronet to reconfigure.

Conquering Our Emotional Body and Conquering Ourself

You have to want to do this. You have to want to conquer yourself. The Bel Shanai said to me when she gave me the sword when I was a young man, "Here, Ram, go and conquer yourself." Conquering myself meant exactly what I am teaching you today, and I went about it unplugging my hate, anger, bitterness, and ignorance and replugged them into nature. Over the years my energy moved from outrage to enlightenment in one lifetime. But I wanted it.

You have to want to do this. Just like where I went to the trunk and was pulling out the garment of doubt, I really didn't want to give that to the vision because I wanted to have a little power. I want to be able to unplug the doubt, and if I give the vision my doubt, then I give it my power. That is the nittus-grittus of protecting your humanity. Doubt is a sword that you carry. You can cut anything up with it that you want and it will be utterly acceptable to do so. But not until I throw it in am I free of it, and only when I no longer doubt can I become the wind.

Now I am going to conclude with an explanation about emotions, that emotions are what we call the emotional body contained within the physical body. After the teaching on the brain you begin to understand that emotion is cell reflex according to neuropathway firing. Simple, except it doesn't look so good on a greeting card, "You reflexed my cells."

You now see that we have in the human drama a dilemma that is problematic in the sense that the brain's need to take care of the body is based on its need to keep it surviving. Under the auspices of survival, the foundation of the personality springs these various emotions, and they do have varying degrees only because they are slightly altered and different in their nerve centers or their neuronet. Remember that the axon of a nerve cell can be three to four feet long. We begin to see then that with these bundles of nerves coming in from the thalamus at the door and then moving all the way through down the body, that each neuronet in the brain causes a muscular or cellular reflex in the body.

When it does that, if you are having a tantrum of anger then your brain is firing according to its environment a repulse of something that happened. What that causes is a fight/flight syndrome to occur in the body. The emotion of anger prepares the body for fight or flight, and it does so by causing the nerves to reflex muscles, tendons, to cause the adrenals to start pouring into the bloodstream the adrenal hormones that allow that which is termed the closing down of the intestinal processes, forcing all the blood to the muscles for an emotional defense. So the emotional body then is tied into each one of these neuronet programs, and the program itself is a code. The body can't help it. As soon as the body gets these signals from the brain, they have to respond accordingly. Your heart starts beating in rapid succession. You start gripping. You start getting into a state of tenseness and stress because your body is responding to the brain's emotional neuropathway.

The body is the recipient of this brain up here that is also projecting a hologram. Not only is this hologram casting the future destiny that you are going to experience but it is causing a delayed reaction in the physical body. When I say to you that the body lives in the past, we see that what is occurring up here in the present is occurring over here in the future, and the last to receive it is the body. Long after you have stopped being mad, your body is still sweating. We call this the emotional body.

With each one of these neuronets, there is a particular degree of physical response required: crying, anger, stress, happiness. You all know the feelings well. When a person gets into what is called an emotional cycle, what that means is a person is set off by something in their environment that starts pushing one of these buttons. Those buttons start to fire. That in turn causes a physical response to occur in the body. The physical response can be crying, depression, anger, or erratic behavior. In the meantime this neuronet up here has cast the infrared shadow to the future. While you are in an emotional state, as days pass you now start to experience what you created two days prior, and then that causes you to be even more upset. What is it called? When it rains, it pours. This is the cycle.

So why are you crying and why are you depressed? You did it. Change it. Why can't you stop crying? If you don't stop, you are only going to continue the cycle. Furthermore, you are going to create a grievous future.

What is going to happen to you if you don't unplug this trauma is that this body that lives in the past is going to get so tired of shutting down its cell-site receptors to nutrients — because it is starving in order to fight — that everything you feed it, it refuses to eat so it stores it as fat. What is going to happen is that body is going to break down and die, and every disease that is already in you as a potential is going to flourish in the body because the body is now living in an acid-based environment.

When a person is depressed, it is because they are caught in a neuronet emotional cycle that they keep creating their future with every day. It is inexcusable to any master in this school to have that continue, knowing what you know.

A Master's Moral Duty:
Applying the Knowledge into Practice

Knowing what you know, if you do not apply it then you are not worthy of being called a master because you have been given the knowledge as well as the wisdom to be able to create a new paradigm and focus on it. Understand that your body is going to weep for another day, but the new thought is being formed and it is being formed by you. When the emotional body has settled down, the neuronet of that emotion has been unplugged. Then you don't have to go around looking for what caused it. The cause is in you. When you correct the cause, the environment will adjust.

If you don't apply what you have learned here, you are not worthy to be called a master because all of this knowledge that I have taught you, as fabulous as it is, will then only remain an empty philosophy to you. If you are no greater than your next meal, then you have lost the game in life because you have abolished your Spirit in favor of your humanity. Furthermore, there is no one, no matter what body you were born in, that should ever accept your body as the ultimate destiny of this life cycle, because if you do you are not a spiritual master. You are just merely a human being giving lip service to fabulous wisdom and not applying it.

No one is as they were born to be, no one. Everyone here can change not only the genetics that are influencing their daily life but they can change their behavior, thereby altering their DNA and changing their body. No one should say to me, "I am what I am," because everyone here now has the capacity to change their life.

I have always found it interesting that being a warlord in my time, as it were, I liked to destroy the environment so it would look the way I wanted it to look. My enlightenment came when I destroyed my inner environment and left the outer alone, and it became quite beautiful.

People like to destroy their world and modify it according to how they think they are. "Well, I am just this way. That is the way God made me."

I am not impressed. You should never show your ignorance. Those sorts of people want to declare war on their environment, on nature. They want to make war on creation to fit them, so they run around there with a sword neutering all of life. They are carving it out to reflect them. It hasn't occurred to them that they need to change, and when they do, the environment will change. These people that say, "Well, God made me the way that I am, so thereby I am going to go out and make everything the way that I want it to be" are impoverished in Spirit; moreover, not a master at all.

If you settle for your humanity, you starve to death your Spirit. If you settle for your body, as the final act it is going to die and go to the grave and you are going to be reborn again, and God knows what the next vehicle will look like. If you don't start becoming more spiritual and less physical, then your chances of survival are nil.

When you become a spiritual person, you do not live from lack but you are abundance. When you are a spiritual person, there is no such thing as insecurity; there is only life. When you are a spiritual person, there is no such thing as good and bad; there is only evolution. When you are a spiritual person, you don't have to depend upon other people making you feel good, because there is no room for that in the Spirit. When you are a spiritual person, you will be shocked and amazed at how brilliant your mind will become. The day you become a human person, you will be shocked and dismayed at wondering where the brilliance went.

No one should use their body as an excuse for their behavior. We are going to learn to change and to be greater than the physical apparatus that we have inhabited, and by our grace we will change it to be an immortal thing instead of a passing thing. The day that you are not so concerned about what you look like but what you think like is the day I will be impressed. So be it.

These teachings will be released and I feel that we should call them "The Neuronet to the Levitating Buddha," and the second part, "The Flower of a Thousand Petals: The Resolve to Human Conflict."

Tonight, before you go to bed, I want you to create your tomorrow. I want you to see yourself arising in joy, being ecstatic about what the day brings, being able to apply all your knowledge you have learned, and being overjoyed that you are finding truth in it and it actually works and that there really is a way to become greater than your lower self. Create that for tomorrow. It just may happen.

Until then, you should know that I have a crush on you, that I adore you and love you and will celebrate the day to where everything I say you are in common agreement with. So be it. That is all.

— *Ramtha*

Epilogue: Metagrams — A Secret Language of the Brain

Ramtha: You have learned tonight?

Music: Yes.

Ramtha: You like what you heard? I could not contain myself.

Music: I didn't know that increasing loudness would change the frequency.

Ramtha: Of course it does.

Music: I know that when you hit a note on the piano, that as it softens off, there is a bend in the harmonic. But taking one note and playing it and then the same note just louder, would it be like C, D, E, F, and G would be like Hertzian and infrared? (Ramtha sings the theme notes from the movie, *Close Encounters of the Third Kind*.)[9] But those are five different harmonics. They are pitches.

Ramtha: But were they not played loudly?

Music: Yes.

Ramtha: You see, there is a point to where it is so loud that you no longer hear it. Loudness is really just an example. Everyone can understand tone but no one can understand invisibility. If we take a tone to its highest level, its loudest level, it will disappear.

Music: But doesn't it change in pitch?

Ramtha: Never.

Music: When you were doing your little example, you raised your pitch even when you went through that. So frequency isn't raising pitch; it is raising volume?

Ramtha: Yes. But how many frequencies are there?

Music: Well, they are innumerable.

Ramtha: Exactly. So each one of them have a high and low end.

---

9 *Close Encounters of the Third Kind* (Columbia Pictures: Richard Dreyfuss, François Truffaut, 1977).

Music: And that all equates to volume?

Ramtha: Volume, not so much sound but its ability to broadcast energy. Use sound as a metaphor.

Music: So my little B-flat in the subliminals is very low.[10] How can it have much of an effect?

Ramtha: It has a great effect because it is most effective by not being loud, entity. It is slowing the rhythm of acceptance.

Music: I see.

Ramtha: So be it.

Music: And the other thing that confused me was when you did the waves on the board. What I know is that tighter waves equals higher frequency, and then the looser the wave, the lower the frequency. So you drew a tight wave and then a loose wave, but then you explained that it went higher in frequency, but that was a lower wave.

Ramtha: How do you know?

Music: Well, it was a looser band. There was more space.

Ramtha: Entity, if we took those and collapsed them like an accordion together, it would be the same frequency. It would just be different. One day you will understand what I was endeavoring to teach today, because most people get hung up with linear expressions of things when they have to understand that everything in containment is existing simultaneously in all different time. So how do we move B-flat to the twelfth dimension and it is still B-flat?

Music: By increasing its volume.

Ramtha: Increasing its frequency.

Music: But there is a point where the higher the pitch goes here, we can't hear with the human ear.

Ramtha: And there is also the lower you go, you cannot hear either.

Music: So what is the difference?

10 *Ancient Echo with "The List" Subliminals* (Yelm: Majestic Productions, 1995) and *The List on the Deschutes River with Frog Chorus* (Yelm: Ramtha's School of Enlightenment, 2005).

Ramtha: B-flat can be played in such a way that it cannot be heard either. All the notes can be.

Music: I really want to understand. I know what a harmonic is. I know what frequency is. I know what notes are, but I don't understand them.

Ramtha: Why don't you focus on this?

Music: All the books that I have tried to get and read are so over my head because they are so mathematical.

Ramtha: Oh, forget that. I will send you a runner. In the meantime you think about this, that every note you play can exist simultaneously in multiple times. Now from what you have been taught, in order to do that then its frequency would have to change in order to exist in a different time. Remember how we did the pyramid coming down and we are rolling up atmosphere, we are stretching it, and because we are stretching it, it rolls up because it is actually of a different time than the slower time we are putting it into. Imagine B-flat on all seven levels, but it would still be B-flat. Think of it that way. And if you will let your mind go, then you will understand what I was doing on the board tonight.

Music: I know that when I play music, the louder I play music in the arena the more it becomes everything in the arena.

Ramtha: Exactly.

Music: So I understand how it would be the overriding frequency in the arena and how it can catch everybody up into that.

Ramtha: Exactly.

Music: So when you put the harmonic like (theme notes from Close Encounters of the Third Kind), what are those five notes? Why does the sequence of certain notes make the different shapes in the brain? What makes the pentagrams? You said that Mozart's music and Tchaikovsky's —

Ramtha: Yes, they are a secret language in the brain. They cause the brain to form certain metagrams. A metagram is a hologram induced by sound. So when they do that, they are actually creating a symbolic destiny that is going to occur to the listener, but the listener doesn't know that. The message comes in the form of a harmonic, that when the harmonic resonates with levels of neurons, those neurons fire to form these sacred patterns.

We discussed tonight that all of the neurons phase differently. So there will be different sounds. There will be different frequencies of B-flat that will cause different neurons to respond. The same neuron for B-flat is not going to respond to it in the high band as it will in the low band. Do you understand?

Music: Yes, but is that not changing octaves of B-flat?

Ramtha: No. It is what you think it is. But if we are talking about a multiple time, then an octave would have nothing to do with changing its octave here but its time-relative space somewhere else. The neurons in the brain know how to fire that code. So think of the neuron fingers as keys to a keyboard.

Music: How would I find out what harmonics would create those patterns?

Ramtha: Why don't you focus on it. Doesn't consciousness and energy create the nature of reality?

Music: Yes.

Ramtha: And, furthermore, didn't I tell you tonight that the gaining and acquisition of knowledge is what brings about a greater reality? So what if you then put that forth into the question, what kind of knowledge will come your way? Lots.

Music: So be it.

Ramtha: So be it, Master of Music.

EPILOGUE BY JZ KNIGHT: HOW IT ALL STARTED

"In other words, his whole point of focus is to come here and to teach you to be extraordinary."

My name is JZ Knight and I am the rightful owner of this body. Ramtha and I are two different people, two different beings. We have a common reality point and that is usually my body. Though we sort of look the same, we really don't look the same.

All of my life, ever since I was a little person, I have heard voices in my head and I have seen wonderful things that to me in my life were normal. I was fortunate enough to have a mother who was a very psychic human being and never condemned what it was that I was seeing. I had wonderful experiences all my life but the most important experience was that I had this deep and profound love for God and there was a part of me that understood what that was. Later in my life I went to church and I tried to understand God from the viewpoint of religious doctrine and had a lot of difficulty with that because it was sort of in conflict with what I felt and what I knew.

Ramtha has been a part of my life ever since I was born, but I didn't know who he was and I didn't know what he was, only that there was a wonderful force that walked with me, and when I was in trouble — and I had a lot of pain in my life growing up — that I always had extraordinary experiences with this being who would talk to me. I could hear him as clearly as I can hear you if we were to have a conversation. He helped me to understand a lot of things in my life that were beyond the normal scope of what someone would give someone as advice.

It wasn't until 1977 that he appeared to me in my kitchen on a Sunday afternoon as I was making pyramids with my husband. We were dehydrating food because we were into hiking and backpacking. As I put one of these ridiculous things on my head, at the other end of my kitchen this wonderful apparition appeared that was seven feet tall and glittery and beautiful and stark. You just don't expect at 2:30 in the afternoon that this is going to appear in your kitchen. No one is ever prepared for that. So Ramtha at that time really made his appearance known to me.

The first thing I said to him — and I don't know where this came from — was, "You are so beautiful. Who are you?" He has a smile like the sun. He is extraordinarily handsome. He said, "My name is Ramtha the Enlightened One and I have come to help you over the ditch." Being the simple person that I am, my immediate reaction was to look at the floor because I thought maybe something had happened to the floor, or the bomb was being dropped. I didn't know. From that day forward he became a constant in my life. And during the year of 1977 a lot of interesting things happened, to say the least. My two younger children at that time got to meet Ramtha and got to experience some incredible phenomena, as well as my husband.

Later that year, after teaching me and having some difficulty telling me what he was and me understanding, one day he said to me, "I am going to send you a runner that will bring you a set of books, and you read them because then you will know what I am." Those books were called the *Life and Teaching of the Masters of the Far East* (DeVorss & Co. Publishers, 1964). I read them and I began to understand that Ramtha was one of those beings, in a way, and that took me out of the are-you-the-devil-or-are-you-God sort of category that was plaguing me at the time.

After I got to understand him he spent long, long moments walking into my living room, all seven feet of this beautiful being, making himself comfortable on my couch, sitting down and talking to me and teaching me. What I didn't realize at that particular time was he already knew all the things I was going to ask and he already knew how to answer them, but I didn't know that he knew that.

Since 1977 he patiently dealt with me in a manner that allowed me to question not his authenticity but things about myself as God, teaching me, catching me when I would get caught up in dogma or get caught up in limitation, catching me just in time and teaching me and walking me through that. And I always said, "You know, you are so patient. I think it is wonderful that you are so patient." And he would just smile and say that he is 35,000 years old, what else can you do in that period of time? It wasn't until about ten years ago that I realized that he already knew what I was going to ask and that is why he was so patient. But as the grand teacher that he is, he allowed me the opportunity to address these issues in myself. He had the grace to speak to me in a way that was not presumptuous but, as a true teacher, would allow me to come to realizations on my own.

Channeling Ramtha since late 1979 has been an experience. Ram is seven feet tall and he wears two robes that I have always seen him in. Even though they are the same robe, they are really beautiful so you never get tired of seeing them. The inner robe is snow white and goes all the way down to where I presume his feet are, and then he has an overrobe that is beautiful purple. You should understand that I have really looked at the material on these robes and it is not really material; it is sort of like light. And though the light has a transparency to them, there is an understanding that what he is wearing has a reality to it.

Ramtha's face is cinnamon-colored skin, and that is the best way I can describe it. It is not really brown and it is not really white and it is not really red. It is sort of a blending of that. He has very deep black eyes that can look into you, and you know you are being looked into. He has eyebrows that look like wings of a bird that come high on his brow. He has a very square jaw and a beautiful mouth, and when he smiles you know that you are in heaven. He

71

has long, long hands and long fingers that he uses very eloquently to demonstrate his thought.

Imagine then after he taught me to get out of my body by actually pulling me out, throwing me in the tunnel, hitting the wall of light and bouncing back — and realizing my kids were home from school and I just got through doing breakfast dishes — that getting used to missing time on this plane was really difficult. I didn't understand what I was doing and where I was going, so we had a lot of practice sessions. You have to understand that he did this to me at ten o'clock in the morning and when I came back off of the white wall it was 4:30. I had a real problem trying to adjust with the time that was missing here. So we had a long time with Ramtha teaching me how to do that, and it was fun and frolic and absolutely terrifying at moments. You can imagine if he walked up to you, yanked you right out of your body, threw you up to the ceiling and said, "Now what does that view look like?" and then throwing you in a tunnel — and perhaps the best way to describe it is it is a black hole into the next level — and being flung through this tunnel and hitting this white wall and having amnesia.

What he was getting me ready to do was to teach me something that I had already agreed to prior to this incarnation. My destiny in this life was not just to marry and to have children and to do well in life but to overcome the adversity to let what was previously planned happen, and that happening included an extraordinary consciousness, which he is.

Trying to dress my body for Ramtha was a joke. I didn't know what to do. The first time we had a channeling session I wore heels and a skirt. I thought I was going to church. So you can imagine, if you have a little time to study him, how he would appear dressed up in a business suit with heels on, which he never walked in in his life.

It is really difficult to talk to people and have them

understand that I am not him, that we are two separate beings and that when you talk to me in this body, you are talking to me and not him. Sometimes over the past decade or so, that has been a great challenge to me in the public media because people don't understand how it is possible that a human being can be endowed with a divine mind and yet be separate from it.

I wanted you to know that although you see Ramtha out here in my body, it is my body, but he doesn't look anything like this. His appearance in the body doesn't lessen the magnitude of who and what he is. You should also know that when we do talk, when you start asking me about things that he said, I may not have a clue what you are talking about because when I leave my body, I am gone to a whole other time and another place that I don't have cognizant memory of. And however long he spends with you, to me that will be maybe about five minutes or three minutes. And when I come back to my body, this whole time of this whole day has passed and I wasn't a part of it. I didn't hear what he said to you and I don't know what he did out here. When I come back, my body is exhausted. It is hard to get up the stairs sometimes to change my clothes and make myself more presentable for what the day is bringing me, or what is left of the day.

He has shown me a lot of wonderful things that I suppose people who have never gotten to see couldn't even dream of in their wildest dreams. I have seen the twenty-third universe and I have met extraordinary beings and I have seen life come and go. I have watched generations be born and live and pass in a matter of moments. I have been exposed to historical events to help me understand better what it was I needed to know. I have been allowed to walk beside my body in other lifetimes and watch how I was and who I was, and I have been allowed to see the other side of death. These are cherished and privileged opportunities that somewhere in my life I earned the right to have them. To speak of them to other people is, in a way, disenchanting because it is difficult to convey to people who have never been to those places what it is. I try my best as a storyteller to tell them and still fall short of it.

I also know that the reason that he works with his students the way that he does is because Ramtha never wants to overshadow any of you. In other words, his whole point of focus is to come here and to teach you to be extraordinary. He already is. And it is not about him producing phenomena. If he told you he was going to send you runners, you are going to get them big time. It is not about him doing tricks in front of you. That is not what he is. Those are tools of an avatar that is still a guru that needs to be worshiped, and that is not the case with him.

So what will happen is he will teach you and cultivate you and allow you to create the phenomenon, and you will be able to do that. Then one day when you are able to manifest on cue and you are able to leave your body and you are able to love, when it is to the human interest impossible to do that, he will walk right out here in your life because you are ready to share what he is. And what he is is simply what you are going to become. Until then he is diligent, patient, all-knowing, and all-understanding of everything that we need to know in order to learn to be that.

The one thing I can say to you is that if you are interested in his presentation, and you are starting to love him even though you can't see him, that is a good sign because it means that what was important in you was your soul urging you to unfold in this lifetime. And it may be against your neuronet. Your personality can argue with you and debate with you, but that sort of logic is really transparent when the soul urges you onto an experience.

If this is what you want to do, you are going to have to exercise patience and focus and you are going to have to do the work. The work in the beginning is very hard, but if you have the tenacity to stay with it, then one day I can tell you that this teacher is going to turn you inside out. One day you will be able to do all the remarkable things that you have heard the masters in myth and legend have the capacity to do. You will be able to do them because that is the journey. And ultimately that ability is singularly the reality of a God awakening in human form.

Now that is my journey and it has been my journey all of my life. If it wasn't important and if it wasn't what it was, I certainly wouldn't be living in oblivion most of the year for the sake of having a few people come to have a New Age experience. This is far greater than a New Age experience. I should also say that it is far more important than the ability to meditate or the ability to do yoga. It is about changing consciousness all through our lives on every point and to be able to unhinge and unlimit our minds so that we can be all we can be.

You should also know what I have learned is that we can only demonstrate what we are capable of demonstrating. If you would say, well, what is blocking me from doing that, the only block that we have is our inability to surrender, to allow, and to support ourself even in the face of our own neuronet of doubt. If you can support yourself through doubt, then you will make the breakthrough because that is the only block that stands in your way. And one day you are going to do all these things and get to see all the things that I have seen and been allowed to see.

So I just wanted to come out here and show you that I exist, that I love what I do, and that I hope that you are learning from this teacher. And, more importantly, I hope you continue with it.

— *JZ Knight*

Ramtha's Glossary

Analogical. Being analogical means living in the Now. It is the creative moment and is outside of time, the past, and the emotions.

Analogical mind. Analogical mind means one mind. It is the result of the alignment of primary consciousness and secondary consciousness, the Observer and the personality. The fourth, fifth, sixth, and seventh seals of the body are opened in this state of mind. The bands spin in opposite directions, like a wheel within a wheel, creating a powerful vortex that allows the thoughts held in the frontal lobe to coagulate and manifest.

Bands, the. The bands are the two sets of seven frequencies that surround the human body and hold it together. Each of the seven frequency layers of each band corresponds to the seven seals of seven levels of consciousness in the human body. The bands are the auric field that allow the processes of binary and analogical mind.

Binary mind. This term means two minds. It is the mind produced by accessing the knowledge of the human personality and the physical body without accessing our deep subconscious mind. Binary mind relies solely on the knowledge, perception, and thought processes of the neocortex and the first three seals. The fourth, fifth, sixth, and seventh seals remain closed in this state of mind.

Blue Body®. It is the body that belongs to the fourth plane of existence, the bridge consciousness, and the ultraviolet frequency band. The Blue Body® is the lord over the lightbody and the physical plane.

Blue Body® Dance. It is a discipline taught by Ramtha in which the students lift their conscious awareness to the consciousness of the fourth plane. This discipline allows the Blue Body® to be accessed and the fourth seal to be opened.

Blue Body® Healing. It is a discipline taught by Ramtha in which the students lift their conscious awareness to the consciousness of the fourth plane and the Blue Body® for the purpose of healing or changing the physical body.

Blue webs. The blue webs represent the basic structure at a subtle level of the physical body. It is the invisible skeletal structure of the physical realm vibrating at the level of ultraviolet frequency.

Body/mind consciousness. Body/mind consciousness is the consciousness that belongs to the physical plane and the human body.

Book of Life. Ramtha refers to the soul as the Book of Life, where the whole journey of involution and evolution of each individual is recorded in the form of wisdom.

C&E® = R. Consciousness and energy create the nature of reality.

C&E®. Abbreviation of Consciousness & Energy℠. This is the service mark of the fundamental discipline of manifestation and the raising of consciousness taught in Ramtha's School of Enlightenment. Through this discipline the students learn to create an analogical state of mind, open up their higher seals, and create reality from the Void. A Beginning C&E® Workshop is the name of the Introductory Workshop for beginning students in which they learn the fundamental concepts and disciplines of Ramtha's teachings. The teachings of the Beginning C&E® Workshop can be found in *Ramtha, A Beginner's Guide to Creating Reality,* third ed. (Yelm: JZK Publishing, a division of JZK, Inc., 2004), and in *Ramtha, Creating Personal Reality*, Tape 380 ed. (Yelm: Ramtha Dialogues, 1998).

Christwalk. The Christwalk is a discipline designed by Ramtha in which the student learns to walk very slowly being acutely aware. In this discipline the students learn to manifest, with each step they take, the mind of a Christ.

Consciousness. Consciousness is the child who was born from the Void's contemplation of itself. It is the essence and fabric of all being. Everything that exists originated in consciousness and manifested outwardly through its handmaiden energy. A stream of consciousness refers to the continuum of the mind of God.

Consciousness and energy. Consciousness and energy are the dynamic force of creation and are inextricably combined. Everything that exists originated in consciousness and manifested through the modulation of its energy impact into mass.

Create Your DaySM. This is the service mark for a technique created by Ramtha for raising consciousness and energy and intentionally creating a constructive plan of experiences and events for the day early in the morning before the start of the day. This technique is exclusively taught at Ramtha's School of Enlightenment.

Disciplines of the Great Work. Ramtha's School of Ancient Wisdom is dedicated to the Great Work. The disciplines of the Great Work practiced in Ramtha's School of Enlightenment are all designed in their entirety by Ramtha. These practices are powerful initiations where the student has the opportunity to apply and experience firsthand the teachings of Ramtha.

Emotional body. The emotional body is the collection of past emotions, attitudes, and electrochemical patterns that make up the brain's neuronet and define the human personality of an individual. Ramtha describes it as the seduction of the unenlightened. It is the reason for cyclical reincarnation.

Emotions. An emotion is the physical, biochemical effect of an experience. Emotions belong to the past, for they are the expression of experiences that are already known and mapped in the neuropathways of the brain.

Energy. Energy is the counterpart of consciousness. All consciousness carries with it a dynamic energy impact, radiation, or natural expression of itself. Likewise, all forms of energy carry with it a consciousness that defines it.

Enlightenment. Enlightenment is the full realization of the human person, the attainment of immortality, and unlimited mind. It is the result of raising the kundalini energy sitting at the base of the spine to the seventh seal that opens the dormant parts of the brain. When the energy penetrates the lower cerebellum and the midbrain, and the subconscious mind is opened, the individual experiences a blinding flash of light called enlightenment.

Evolution. Evolution is the journey back home from the slowest levels of frequency and mass to the highest levels of consciousness and Point Zero.

FieldworkSM. FieldworkSM is one of the fundamental disciplines of Ramtha's School of Enlightenment. The students are taught to create a symbol of something they want to know and experience and draw it on a paper card. These cards are placed with the blank side facing out on the fence rails of a large field. The students blindfold themselves and focus on their symbol, allowing their body to walk freely to find their card through the application of the law of consciousness and energy and analogical mind.

Fifth plane. The fifth plane of existence is the plane of superconsciousness and x-ray frequency. It is also known as the Golden Plane or paradise.

Fifth seal. This seal is the center of our spiritual body that connects us to the fifth plane. It is associated with the thyroid gland and with speaking and living the truth without dualism.

First plane. It refers to the material or physical plane. It is the plane of the image consciousness and Hertzian frequency. It is the slowest and densest form of coagulated consciousness and energy.

First seal. The first seal is associated with the reproductive organs, sexuality, and survival.

First three seals. The first three seals are the seals of sexuality, pain and suffering, and controlling power. These are the seals commonly at play in all of the complexities of the human drama.

Fourth plane. The fourth plane of existence is the realm of the bridge consciousness and ultraviolet frequency. This plane is described as the plane of Shiva, the destroyer of the old and creator of the new. In this plane, energy is not yet split into positive and negative polarity. Any lasting changes or healing of the physical body must be changed first at the level of the fourth plane and the Blue Body®. This plane is also called the Blue Plane, or the plane of Shiva.

Fourth seal. The fourth seal is associated with unconditional love and the thymus gland. When this seal is activated, a hormone is released that maintains the body in perfect health and stops the aging process.

God. Ramtha's teachings are an exposition of the statement, "You are God." Humanity is described as the forgotten Gods, divine beings by nature who have forgotten their heritage and true identity. It is precisely this statement that represents Ramtha's challenging message to our modern age, an age riddled with religious superstition and misconceptions about the divine and the true knowledge of wisdom.

God within. It is the Observer, the great self, the primary consciousness, the Spirit, the God within the human person.

God/man. The full realization of a human being.

God/woman. The full realization of a human being.

Gods. The Gods are technologically advanced beings from other star systems who came to Earth 455,000 years ago. These Gods manipulated the human race genetically, mixing and modifying our DNA with theirs. They are responsible for the evolution of the neocortex and used the human race as a subdued work force. Evidence of these events is recorded in the Sumerian tablets and artifacts. This term is also used to describe the true identity of humanity, the forgotten Gods.

Golden body. It is the body that belongs to the fifth plane, superconsciousness, and x-ray frequency.

Great Work. The Great Work is the practical application of the knowledge of the Schools of Ancient Wisdom. It refers to the disciplines by which the human person becomes enlightened and is transmuted into an immortal, divine being.

Grid^SM, The. This is the service mark for a technique created by Ramtha for raising consciousness and energy and intentionally tapping into the Zero Point Energy field and the fabric of reality through a mental visualization. This technique is exclusively taught at Ramtha's School of Enlightenment.

Hierophant. A hierophant is a master teacher who is able to manifest what they teach and initiate their students into such knowledge.

Hyperconsciousness. Hyperconsciousness is the consciousness of the sixth plane and gamma ray frequency.

Infinite Unknown. It is the frequency band of the seventh plane of existence and ultraconsciousness.

Involution. Involution is the journey from Point Zero and the seventh plane to the slowest and densest levels of frequency and mass.

JZ Knight. JZ Knight is the only person appointed by Ramtha to channel him. Ramtha refers to JZ as his beloved daughter. She was Ramaya, the eldest of the children given to Ramtha during his lifetime.

Kundalini. Kundalini energy is the life force of a person that descends from the higher seals to the base of the spine at puberty. It is a large packet of energy reserved for human evolution, commonly pictured as a coiled serpent that sits at the base of the spine. This energy is different from the energy coming out of the first three seals responsible for sexuality, pain and suffering, power, and victimization. It is commonly described as the sleeping serpent or the sleeping dragon. The journey of the kundalini energy to the crown of the head is called the journey of enlightenment. This journey takes place when this serpent wakes up and starts to split and dance around the spine, ionizing the spinal fluid and changing its molecular structure. This action causes the opening of the midbrain and the door to the subconscious mind.

Life force. The life force is the Father/Mother, the Spirit, the breath of life within the person that is the platform from which the person creates its illusions, imagination, and dreams.

Life review. It is the review of the previous incarnation that occurs when the person reaches the third plane after death. The person gets the opportunity to be the Observer, the actor, and the recipient of its own actions. The unresolved issues from that lifetime that emerge at the life or light review set the agenda for the next incarnation.

Light, the. The light refers to the third plane of existence.

Lightbody. It is the same as the radiant body. It is the body that belongs to the third plane of conscious awareness and the visible light frequency band.

List, the. The List is the discipline taught by Ramtha where the student gets to write a list of items they desire to know and experience and then learn to focus on it in an analogical state of consciousness. The List is the map used to design, change, and reprogram the neuronet of the person. It is the tool that helps to bring meaningful and lasting changes in the person and their reality.

Make known the unknown. This phrase expresses the original divine mandate given to the Source consciousness to manifest and bring to conscious awareness all of the infinite potentials of the Void. This statement represents the basic intent that inspires the dynamic process of creation and evolution.

Mind. Mind is the product of streams of consciousness and energy acting on the brain creating thought-forms, holographic segments, or neurosynaptic patterns called memory. The streams of consciousness and energy are what keep the brain alive. They are its power source. A person's ability to think is what gives them a mind.

Mind of God. The mind of God comprises the mind and wisdom of every lifeform that ever lived on any dimension, in any time, or that ever will live on any planet, any star, or region of space.

Mirror consciousness. When Point Zero imitated the act of contemplation of the Void it created a mirror reflection of itself, a point of reference that made the exploration of the Void possible. It is called mirror consciousness or secondary consciousness. See **Self.**

Monkey-mind. Monkey-mind refers to the flickering, swinging mind of the personality.

Mother/Father Principle. It is the source of all life, the Father, the eternal Mother, the Void. In Ramtha's teachings, the Source and God the creator are not the same. God the creator is seen as Point Zero and primary consciousness but not as the Source, or the Void, itself.

Name-field. The name-field is the name of the large field where the discipline of Fieldwork℠ is practiced.

Neighborhood Walk℠. This is the service mark of a technique created by JZ Knight for raising consciousness and energy and intentionally modifying our neuronets and set patterns of thinking no longer wanted and replacing them with new ones of our choice. This technique is exclusively taught at Ramtha's School of Enlightenment.

Neuronet. The contraction for "neural network," a network of neurons that perform a function together.

Observer. It refers to the Observer responsible for collapsing the particle/wave of quantum mechanics. It represents the great self, the Spirit, primary consciousness, the God within the human person.

Outrageous. Ramtha uses this word in a positive way to express something or someone who is extraordinary and unusual, unrestrained in action, and excessively bold or fierce.

People, places, things, times, and events. These are the main areas of human experience to which the personality is emotionally attached. These areas represent the past of the human person and constitute the content of the emotional body.

Personality, the. See **Emotional body.**

Plane of Bliss. It refers to the plane of rest where souls get to plan their next incarnations after their life reviews. It is also known as heaven and paradise where there is no suffering, no pain, no need or lack, and where every wish is immediately manifested.

Plane of demonstration. The physical plane is also called the plane of demonstration. It is the plane where the person has the opportunity to demonstrate its creative potentiality in mass and witness consciousness in material form in order to expand its emotional understanding.

Point Zero. It refers to the original point of awareness created by the Void through its act of contemplating itself. Point Zero is the original child of the Void, the birth of consciousness.

Primary consciousness. It is the Observer, the great self, the God within the human person.

Ram. Ram is a shorter version of the name Ramtha. Ramtha means the Father.

Ramaya. Ramtha refers to JZ Knight as his beloved daughter. She was Ramaya, the first one to become Ramtha's adopted child during his lifetime. Ramtha found Ramaya abandoned on the steppes of Russia. Many people gave their children to Ramtha during the march as a gesture of love and highest respect; these children were to be raised in the House of the Ram. His children grew to the great number of 133 even though he never had offspring of his own blood.

Ramtha (etymology). The name of Ramtha the Enlightened One, Lord of the Wind, means the Father. It also refers to the Ram who descended from the mountain on what is known as the terrible day of the Ram. "It is about that in all antiquity. And in ancient Egypt, there is an avenue dedicated to the Ram, the great conqueror. And they were wise enough to understand that whoever could walk down the avenue of the Ram could conquer the wind." The word Aram, the name of Noah's grandson, is formed from the Aramaic noun Araa — meaning earth, landmass — and the word Ramtha, meaning high. This Semitic name echoes Ramtha's descent from the high mountain, which began the great march.

Runner. A runner in Ramtha's lifetime was responsible for bringing specific messages or information. A master teacher has the ability to send runners to other people that manifest their words or intent in the form of an experience or an event.

Second plane. It is the plane of existence of social consciousness and the infrared frequency band. It is associated with pain and suffering. This plane is the negative polarity of the third plane of visible light frequency.

Second seal. This seal is the energy center of social consciousness and the infrared frequency band. It is associated with the experience of pain and suffering and is located in the lower abdominal area.

Secondary consciousness. When Point Zero imitated the act of contemplation of the Void it created a mirror reflection of itself, a point of reference that made the exploration of the Void possible. It is called mirror consciousness or secondary consciousness. See **Self**.

Self, the. The self is the true identity of the human person different from the personality. It is the transcendental aspect of the person. It refers to the secondary consciousness, the traveler in a journey of involution and evolution making known the unknown.

Sending-and-receiving. Sending-and-receiving is the name of the discipline taught by Ramtha in which the student learns to access information using the faculties of the midbrain to the exclusion of sensory perception. This discipline develops the student's psychic ability of telepathy and divination.

Seven seals. The seven seals are powerful energy centers that constitute seven levels of consciousness in the human body. The bands are the way in which the physical body is held together according to these seals. In every human being there is energy spiraling out of the first three seals or centers. The energy pulsating out of the first three seals manifests itself respectively as sexuality, pain, or power. When the upper seals are unlocked, a higher level of awareness is activated.

Seventh plane. The seventh plane is the plane of ultraconsciousness and the Infinite Unknown frequency band. This plane is where the journey of involution began. This plane was created by Point Zero when it imitated the act of contemplation of the Void and the mirror or secondary consciousness was created. A plane of existence or dimension of space and time exists between two points of consciousness. All the other planes were created by slowing down the time and frequency band of the seventh plane.

Seventh seal. This seal is associated with the crown of the head, the pituitary gland, and the attainment of enlightenment.

Shiva. The Lord God Shiva represents the Lord of the Blue Plane and the Blue Body®. Shiva is not used in reference to a singular deity from Hinduism. It is rather the representation of a state of consciousness that belongs to the fourth plane, the ultraviolet frequency band, and the opening of the fourth seal. Shiva is neither male nor female. It is an androgynous being, for the energy of the fourth plane has not yet been split into positive and negative polarity. This is an important distinction from the traditional Hindu representation of Shiva as a male deity who has a wife. The tiger skin at its feet, the trident staff, and the sun and the moon at the level of the head represent the mastery of this body over the first three seals of consciousness. The kundalini energy is pictured as fiery energy shooting from the base of the spine through the head. This is another distinction from some Hindu representations of Shiva with the serpent energy coming out at the level of the fifth seal or throat. Another symbolic image of Shiva is the long threads of dark hair and an abundance of pearl necklaces, which represent its richness of experience owned into wisdom. The quiver and bow and arrows are the agent by which Shiva shoots its powerful will and destroys imperfection and creates the new.

Sixth plane. The sixth plane is the realm of hyperconsciousness and the gamma ray frequency band. In this plane the awareness of being one with the whole of life is experienced.

Sixth seal. This seal is associated with the pineal gland and the gamma ray frequency band. The reticular formation that filters and veils the knowingness of the subconscious mind is opened when this seal is activated. The opening of the brain refers to the opening of this seal and the activation of its consciousness and energy.

Social consciousness. It is the consciousness of the second plane and the infrared frequency band. It is also called the image of the human personality and the mind of the first three seals. Social consciousness refers to the collective consciousness of human society. It is the collection of thoughts, assumptions, judgments, prejudices, laws, morality, values, attitudes, ideals, and emotions of the fraternity of the human race.

Soul. Ramtha refers to the soul as the Book of Life, where the whole journey of involution and evolution of the individual is recorded in the form of wisdom.

Subconscious mind. The seat of the subconscious mind is the lower cerebellum or reptilian brain. This part of the brain has its own independent connections to the frontal lobe and the whole of the body and has the power to access the mind of God, the wisdom of the ages.

Superconsciousness. This is the consciousness of the fifth plane and the x-ray frequency band.

Tahumo. Tahumo is the discipline taught by Ramtha in which the student learns the ability to master the effects of the natural environment — cold and heat — on the human body.

Tank field. It is the name of the large field with the labyrinth that is used for the discipline of The Tank®.

Tank®, The. It is the name given to the labyrinth used as part of the disciplines of Ramtha's School of Enlightenment. The students are taught to find the entry to this labyrinth blindfolded and move through it focusing on the Void without touching the walls or using the eyes or the senses. The objective of this discipline is to find, blindfolded, the center of the labyrinth or a room designated and representative of the Void.

Third plane. This is the plane of conscious awareness and the visible light frequency band. It is also known as the light plane and the mental plane. When the energy of the Blue Plane is lowered down to this frequency band, it splits into positive and negative polarity. It is at this point that the soul splits into two, giving origin to the phenomenon of soulmates.

Third seal. This seal is the energy center of conscious awareness and the visible light frequency band. It is associated with control, tyranny, victimization, and power. It is located in the region of the solar plexus.

Thought. Thought is different from consciousness. The brain processes a stream of consciousness, modifying it into segments — holographic pictures — of neurological, electrical, and chemical prints called thoughts. Thoughts are the building blocks of mind.

Torsion Process^{SM}. This is the service mark of a technique created by Ramtha for raising consciousness and energy and intentionally creating a torsion field using the mind. Through this technique the student learns to build a wormhole in space/time, alter reality, and create dimensional phenomena such as invisibility, levitation, bilocation, teleportation, and others. This technique is exclusively taught at Ramtha's School of Enlightenment.

Twilight®. This term is used to describe the discipline taught by Ramtha in which the students learn to put their bodies in a catatonic state similar to deep sleep, yet retaining their conscious awareness.

Twilight® Visualization Process. It is the process used to practice the discipline of the List or other visualization formats.

Ultraconsciousness. It is the consciousness of the seventh plane and the Infinite Unknown frequency band. It is the consciousness of an ascended master.

Unknown God. The Unknown God was the single God of Ramtha's ancestors, the Lemurians. The Unknown God also represents the forgotten divinity and divine origin of the human person.

Upper four seals. The upper four seals are the fourth, fifth, sixth, and seventh seals.

Void, the. The Void is defined as one vast nothing materially, yet all things potentially. *See* **Mother/Father Principle.**

Yellow brain. The yellow brain is Ramtha's name for the neocortex, the house of analytical and emotional thought. The reason why it is called the yellow brain is because the neocortices were colored yellow in the original two-dimensional, caricature-style drawing Ramtha used for his teaching on the function of the brain and its processes. He explained that the different aspects of the brain in this particular drawing are exaggerated and colorfully highlighted for the sake of study and understanding. This specific drawing became the standard tool used in all the subsequent teachings on the brain.

Yeshua ben Joseph. Ramtha refers to Jesus Christ by the name Yeshua ben Joseph, following the Jewish traditions of that time.

FIG. A: THE SEVEN SEALS:
SEVEN LEVELS OF CONSCIOUSNESS IN THE HUMAN BODY

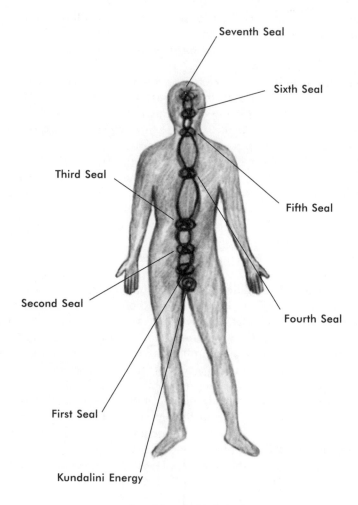

Seventh Seal

Sixth Seal

Third Seal

Fifth Seal

Second Seal

Fourth Seal

First Seal

Kundalini Energy

Fig. B: Seven Levels of Consciousness and Energy

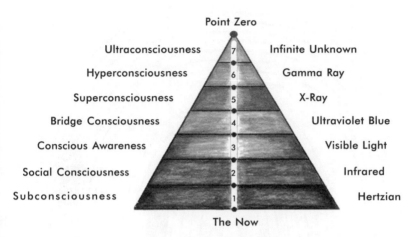

Point Zero

Ultraconsciousness	7	Infinite Unknown
Hyperconsciousness	6	Gamma Ray
Superconsciousness	5	X-Ray
Bridge Consciousness	4	Ultraviolet Blue
Conscious Awareness	3	Visible Light
Social Consciousness	2	Infrared
Subconsciousness	1	Hertzian

The Now

Fig. C: The Brain

Thalamus

Hypothalamus

Frontal Lobe

Pituitary Gland

Hippocampus
and Amygdala

Pons

Reticular
Formation

Neocortex
(The Yellow Brain)

Corpus
Callosum

Midbrain

Pineal
Gland

Lower
Cerebellum

Spinal Cord

Energy

Fig. D: Binary Mind — Living the Image

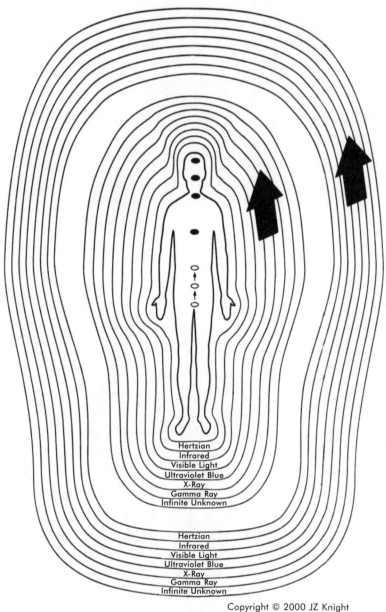

Hertzian
Infrared
Visible Light
Ultraviolet Blue
X-Ray
Gamma Ray
Infinite Unknown

Hertzian
Infrared
Visible Light
Ultraviolet Blue
X-Ray
Gamma Ray
Infinite Unknown

FIG. E: ANALOGICAL MIND — LIVING IN THE NOW

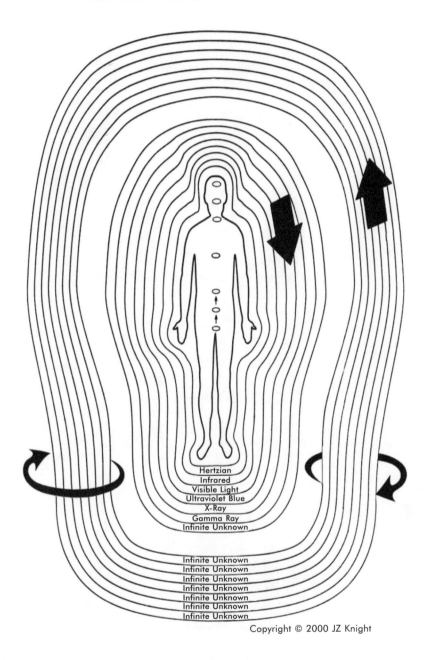

Hertzian
Infrared
Visible Light
Ultraviolet Blue
X-Ray
Gamma Ray
Infinite Unknown

Infinite Unknown
Infinite Unknown
Infinite Unknown
Infinite Unknown
Infinite Unknown
Infinite Unknown
Infinite Unknown

Fig. F: The Observer Effect and the Nerve Cell

The Observer is responsible
for collapsing the wave function of probability
into particle reality.

Particle   Energy wave   The Observer

The act of observation
makes the nerve cells fire and produces thought.

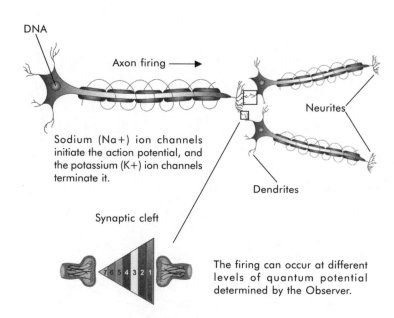

DNA

Axon firing ⟶

Neurites

Sodium (Na+) ion channels
initiate the action potential, and
the potassium (K+) ion channels
terminate it.

Dendrites

Synaptic cleft

7 6 5 4 3 2 1

The firing can occur at different
levels of quantum potential
determined by the Observer.

Fig. G: Cellular Biology and the Thought Connection

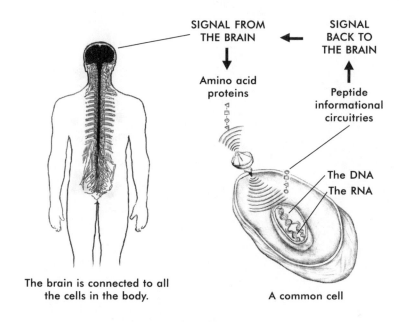

SIGNAL FROM
THE BRAIN

SIGNAL
BACK TO
THE BRAIN

Amino acid
proteins

Peptide
informational
circuitries

The DNA
The RNA

The brain is connected to all
the cells in the body.

A common cell

Ramtha's School of Enlightenment

THE SCHOOL OF ANCIENT WISDOM

A Division of JZK, Inc.
P.O. Box 1210
Yelm, Washington 98597
360.458.5201
800.347.0439
www.ramtha.com
www.jzkpublishing.com